YOUR KNOWLEDGE HA

- We will publish your bachelor's and master's thesis, essays and papers

- Your own eBook and book - sold worldwide in all relevant shops

- Earn money with each sale

Upload your text at www.GRIN.com
and publish for free

Stephanie Scheck

The Stages of Psychosocial Development According to Erik H. Erikson

GRIN Publishing

Bibliographic information published by the German National Library:

The German National Library lists this publication in the National Bibliography; detailed bibliographic data are available on the Internet at http://dnb.dnb.de .

Imprint:

Copyright © 2005 GRIN Verlag GmbH
Print and binding: Books on Demand GmbH, Norderstedt Germany
ISBN: 978-3-656-83770-1

This book at GRIN:

http://www.grin.com/en/e-book/284265/the-stages-of-psychosocial-development-according-to-erik-h-erikson

GRIN - Your knowledge has value

Since its foundation in 1998, GRIN has specialized in publishing academic texts by students, college teachers and other academics as e-book and printed book. The website www.grin.com is an ideal platform for presenting term papers, final papers, scientific essays, dissertations and specialist books.

Visit us on the internet:

http://www.grin.com/

http://www.facebook.com/grincom

http://www.twitter.com/grin_com

Stages of Psychosocial Development According to Erik H. Erikson

Stephanie Scheck

1.   Introduction

Erik H. Erikson (1902 – 1994) is without a doubt one of the most outstanding psychoanalysts of the last century. The native Dane and later US-American further developed the psychosocial aspects and the developmental phases of adulthood in Sigmund Freud's stage theory.

It is Erikson's basic assumption that in the course of a lifetime, the human being goes through eight developmental phases, which are laid out in an internal development plan.

On each level, it is required to solve the relevant crisis, embodied by the integration of opposite poles presenting the development tasks, the successful handling of which is in turn of importance for the following phases.

The term crisis does not have a negative connotation for Erikson, but rather is seen as a state, which through constructive resolution leads to further development, which is being integrated and internalized into the own self-image.

"Each (component) comes to its ascendance, meets its crisis, and finds its lasting solution (...) toward the end of the stages mentioned. All of them exist in the beginning in some form."[1]

Hence, the human development is a process alternating between levels, crises, and the new balance in order to reach increasingly mature stages.

In detail, Erikson studied the possibilities of an individual's advancement and the affective powers that allow it to act. This becomes particularly obvious in the eight psychosocial phases, which now should be the focus of this paper. This demonstrates that Erikson did see development as above all: a lifelong process.

---

[1] ERIKSON, Identity. Youth and crisis, p.95

2. Stages of Psychosocial Development

2.1 Basic trust vs. basic mistrust

In this phase of life, the state of the child is characterized by the trauma of birth. All of a sudden, the child is ripped out of the familiar environment and the bond with the mother is redefined.

The sense of basic trust, defined as "an essential trustfulness"[2], develops during this first phase of life, the first year of life, during the so-called oral stage[3] (Freud), and is, so Erikson, "the cornerstone of a vital personality"[4].

The child learns the simplest and the earliest modality: to "get", not in its negative sense of unsolicited or forcible taking, but in that of accepting what is given[5].

The social reference person is the mother, who through offering the breast not only meets the child's elementary basic needs, like eating, but hereby also provides oral satisfaction. She takes on the role of provider the child can rely on.

The trust is not just depleted in the person of the mother, but according to Erikson it also refers to the infant himself. "By "trust" I mean an essential trustfulness of others as well as a fundamental sense of one's own trustworthiness"[6].

"This forms the very basis in the child for a component of the sense of identity which will later combine a sense of being "alright", of being oneself ..."[7]

This basic trust in oneself and others forms the basis for any later development and consequently is not a stage that has to be overcome, but is something that will always remain and resonate subliminally.

In the second half of the first year of life, according to Erikson, a first crisis does occur.

This crisis appears to consist of the coincidence in time of three developments:

On one part of the physiological, namely that the infant experiences the growing need to absorb, appropriate, and observe things, on the other part of a psychological development, namely the growing realization of being an individual. The third development is dependent on

---

[2] see ERIKSON, Identity. Youth and crisis, p.96
[3] see ERIKSON, Identity. Youth and crisis, p.100
[4] see ERIKSON, Identity. Youth and crisis, p.97
[5] see ERIKSON, Identity. Youth and crisis, p.99
[6] ERIKSON, Identity. Youth and crisis, p.96
[7] ERIKSON, Childhood and Society, p. 249

the environment, as evidently the mother seems to turn away from the child and to focus on other activities.

The child can possibly interpret this turning away as a withdrawal of motherly love.

If a child does not overcome this conflict, and the negative experiences dominate, so according to Erikson, this leads to "(...) acute infantile depression (Spitz, 1945) or to a mild but chronic state of mourning which may give a depressive undertone to the remainder of one's life."[8]

Instead of basic trust, the infant develops basic mistrust.

For this reason, it is important to uphold and strengthen a child's basic trust during this stage, which is connected with increasingly frequent impressions of deceit, separation, and of being abandoned.

The basic attitude that is generated during this first stage of life has an impact on a person's entire life.

If basic trust was built, there is a predominantly optimistic attitude towards other people. If this basic trust is lacking, there is the risk of developing a general basic mistrust, not just towards the world, but also towards oneself. A severely damaged basic trust, or one that is not formed in the first place, can lead to psychic disorders like depression.

The positive experiences, such as feelings of security, warmth, dependability, attentiveness, and devotion should outweigh negative experiences and frustration, such as having to wait for the satisfaction of needs, disappointment, solitude, disregard, or physical pain.

Naturally, frustration cannot be avoided completely in childhood.

According to Erikson it is important, however, that not only positive experiences predominate in order to develop a sense of trust, but that the sum of trust that a child takes away from these early experiences does not absolutely depend on the quantity, but rather the quality of the mother-child-relationship. "Mothers create a sense of trust in their children by that kind of administration which in its quality combines sensitive care of the baby's individual needs and a firm sense of trustworthiness (...)."[9]

Hence, success is rather dependent on the fulfillment of motherly functions within the respective cultural environment and set of values, like knowledge, religion, etc., and not on the quantity of produced motherly love.

---

[8] ERIKSON, Identity. Youth and crisis, p.101
[9] ERIKSON, Identity. Youth and crisis, p.103

So this is the beginning – the coming together of an infant, a pair of parents, and a society, in an act of faith and trust.

2.2   Autonomy vs. shame and doubt

In this second stage, which is the second and third year of life, autonomy is developed with healthy personalities, due to the increasing physical abilities, especially the development of the muscle system. The child is offered two modalities: holding on and letting go.[10] "A general ability, indeed, a violent need, develops to alternate withholding and expelling at will and, in general, to keep tightly and to throw away willfully whatever is held."[11]

The newly acquired ability puts the child in the position to distance himself from the reference person, to set himself apart and to have his will in order to be in a certain way less dependent on the care environment. Moreover, he is able to control bowel and bladder movement on his own.

A particular, however not exclusive role is hereby given to the excretory organs; not without a reason, psychoanalysis has termed this stage the anal phase (Freud).

The ability to control the bodily excretory function means wellbeing for the child, so Erikson. Moreover, control means, at least in Western cultures, praise from the part of reference persons, which "at first must make up for quite frequent discomfort and tension suffered as the bowels learn to do their daily work."[12]

Again, the development of physiological functions goes hand in hand with with the maturation of personal abilities. For the child, controlling the bowel movement is a significant step towards autonomy. By not having to be changed anymore, the child gets more independent from the parents. This strengthens self-confidence, which is supported by acknowledgement given by the parents at the same time.

Erikson calls this entire life stage a "battle for autonomy"[13]. The child begins to compartmentalize his world in "I", "you" and "my"[14]. Erikson includes the seemingly

---

[10] ERIKSON, Identity. Youth and crisis, p.107
[11] ERIKSON, Identity. Youth and crisis, p.107
[12] ERIKSON, Identity. Youth and crisis, p.107
[13] see ERIKSON, Identity. Youth and crisis, p.108
[14] see ERIKSON, Identity. Youth and crisis, p.108

contradictory tendencies, like snuggling and pushing away, picking up and dropping, being obedient and being rebellious under the formula of *"retentive-eliminative modes"*[15].

The special emphasis that in this phase is put on autonomy, however, also makes clear what the child is not able to do yet.

Shame and doubt come up, when aspired goals cannot reached yet and the child has the feeling of being made fun of; this can happen, when for example the process of toilet training is done too strictly or too early. This feeling is being reinforced, when parents prove to be unreliable. In this stage, a balance has to be found between autonomy and dependency.

"In this stage, be firm and yet tolerant towards the child, and he will become firm and tolerant towards himself. He will be proud to be an autonomous person; he will also grant others autonomy; and every now and then he will let something slip for himself."[16]

For the growth of the found autonomy, the child has to be protected from excessive failures that can cause him to feel shame over the own shortcomings, or even to doubt his own competency. Erikson describes shame as "(…) essentially rage turned against the self."[17] and doubt as "the brother of shame"[18].

Therefore it is particularly important, that parenting offers sufficient support for the child and his now awakening thirst for action. The child's needs have to be recognized and taken seriously. Through the approval of his actions and the reaction of reference persons, the child experiences self-confidence and is being reassured and satisfied in his curiosity, his thirst for knowledge and investigation and is thus learning to know and to recognize what he wants. The child develops self-confidence.

The child needs to be encouraged in his actions und should constantly be aware, that the basic trust he gained in the first stage keeps existing.

"The infant must have come to feel that the basic faith in existence, which is the lasting treasure saved from the rages of the oral stage, will not be jeopardized by the violent wish to have his choice, to appropriate demandingly, and to eliminate stubbornly."[19]

This only will allow him to express his will without having to fear, that the parents would disapprove and shame him for his actions. A balance has to be found between autonomy and dependence.

---

[15] see ERIKSON, Identity. Youth and crisis, p.109
[16] ERIKSON, Childhood and Society, p.252
[17] ERIKSON, Childhood and Society, p.252
[18] see ERIKSON, Identity. Youth and crisis, p.112
[19] ERIKSON, Childhood and Society, p.252

However, is the child denied this autonomy by parental authorities, this can in turn lead to fundamental incursions in development and consequently to disorders like compulsive behavior and self-doubt. Individuals who do not develop a sense of autonomy, always harbor doubts and fear criticism.

"For if denied the gradual and well-guided experience of the autonomy of free choice (or if, indeed, weakened by an initial loss of trust) the child will turn against himself all his urge to discriminate and to manipulate. He will over-manipulate himself, he will develop a precocious conscience. Instead of taking possession of things in order to test them by purposeful repetition, he will become obsessed by his own repetitiveness; (...)"[20]

The internalized results of this phase are reflected in the relationship of the individual with the principles of law and order.

2.3   Initiative vs. guilt

The ability to show initiative is at the center of this stage, the fourth and fifth year of life, which corresponds to the oedipal or phallic stage (Freud). In the mastered second stage, the child did learn that he is an individual, convinced to be an independent person. According to Erikson, the child now has to "(...) find out, what kind of a person he may become."[21]

For the first time, he recognizes differences and similarities between himself and other people. Gender differenciation also happens for the first time. The child shifts his focus from himself to the environment and thus begins to explore reality. The child develops scientific curiosity and the motivation to do something, to act, and to approach something.

At this point it appears hardly surprising, that this stage, once more, is characterized by physical abilities. According to Erikson, in this stage the child is helped with three developmental spurts, that however, activate the next crisis: for the first part, the child learns to move around more freely and more violently and therefore establishes a new radius of goals, for the other part his sense of language becomes perfected to the point where he can understand more, can ask questions but also can misunderstand. Both language and locomotion permit him to expand his imagination.[22]

The child then dreams up worlds he cannot avoid frightening himself with.

---

[20] ERIKSON, Childhood and Society, p.252
[21] ERIKSON, Identity. Youth and crisis, p.115
[22] see ERIKSON, Identity. Youth and crisis, p.115

"Nevertheless, out of all this he must emerge with a sense of initiative as a basis for a realistic sense of ambition and purpose."[23]

A resolution of the problem presents itself, when " (...) the child seems to "grow together" both in his person and in his body (...) he is in free possession of a surplus of energy which permits him to forget failures quickly and to approach what seems to be desirable (...) with undimimished and more accurate direction."[24]

The child begins to measure and compare himself with the grownups; he wants to intrude into the adult world, as in general he has an intrusive desire.

The "intrusive mode"[25] dominating much of the behavior of this stage, characterizes a variety of similar activities and fantasies, such as the intrusion into space by vigorous locomotion, the intrusion into other peoples's ears and minds by the aggressive voice, or the intrusion into the unknown by consuming curiosity.

For the reason that the child is trying to understand himself and his world, the interest in his own, yet infantile sexuality is growing[26]. In this area, the child experiences obvious boundaries, due to the lacking physical development; in this context, Erikson mentions the Freudian "Oedipus complex"[27].

With boys, this stage is characterized as phallic and suggests pleasure in attack and conquest. In contrast, in girls this turns to modes of receiving. Their approach is either a more aggressive form of snatching by jealous conquest or the milder form of making oneself "attractive and endearing"[28].

The child basically tries to assume the role of the same-sex parent, while the opposite-sex parent is the target of the seductive behavior. Due to the focus on the environment, the child does not feel rivalry towards younger siblings, but instead towards those who were there first. The child enters the contest for favored position with one of the parents in order to feel resignation, guilt and anxiety with the inevitable failure.

Bound for failure, he is indulging in reenactments and fantasies, because he is not able to defeat the adult and not "mighty" enough to assume their functions.

---

[23] ERIKSON, Identity. Youth and crisis, p.115
[24] ERIKSON, Childhood and Society, p.254
[25] see ERIKSON, Identity. Youth and crisis, p.116
[26] see ERIKSON, Identity. Youth and crisis, p.116
[27] see ERIKSON, Identity. Youth and crisis, p.117
[28] see ERIKSON, Childhood and Society, p.255

"This, then, is the stage of fear for life and limb, of the intensified fear of losing, or on the part oft he girl the conviction that she has lost, the male genital as punishment for secret fantasies and deeds."[29] It is necessary to overcome the castration complex of this stage to get to the realization that the child himself is part of the gender succession.

At the same time, so Erikson, conscience develops during this stage, which he calls "governor of initiative"[30]. Now the child knows already during the act, if he is acting right or wrong and measures himself and the parents by their deeds. The child begins now not only to be ashamed for what he has done, when it is discovered, but he begins to fear the discovery per se and to feel guilty for merely the thought and the actions. Erikson calls this the cornerstone of morality in the individual sense.

The successful handling of the crisis at this stage leads to the child arising from it with an unbroken initiative. If the conflict is not appropriately addressed, it leads to an overzealous conscience, which is also going to hamper and restrict initiative in later stages of life, or to overcompensate. At this stage, a balance has to be found between a healthy dose of initiative and a normal regulation authority.
"The indispensable contribution of the initiative stage to later identity development, then, obviously is that of freeing the child's initiative and sense of purpose for adult tasks which promise (but cannot guarantee) a fulfillment of one's range of capacities."[31]

The result consists of guilt and a feeling to be in charge of the own initiatives.

2.4   Industry vs. inferiority

In this stage, from the sixth year of life up to puberty, there is no new source of inner support and consequently it is also called latency period or stage (Freud)[32], because violent drives of sexual development are temporarily dormant.
Erikson describes this stage also as "(...) a lull before the storm of puberty (...)".[33]

---

[29] ERIKSON, Identity. Youth and crisis, p.119
[30] see ERIKSON, Identity. Youth and crisis, p.119
[31] ERIKSON, Identity. Youth and crisis, p.122
[32] see ERIKSON, Identity. Youth and crisis, p.126
[33] ERIKSON, Identity. Youth and crisis, p.127

If a conviction can summarize the first stage with "I am what hope I have and give", in the second stage with "I am what I can freely", in the third stage with "I am what I can imagine I will", so it is in the fourth stage, that "I am what I can learn to make work"[34] gains priority.

The child is more open to the world and has a growing need to be productive, to learn something new, to contribute to the world of adults, and tob e recognized by it. Erikson calls this desire a "sense of industry"[35].

Erikson does not deny the significance of the play during this stage; he talks about preparing for the future, or a method to vent past agitation, vindicate past failures in his fantasy[36], but also of "a safe place the child creates to return to, if need be to "overhaul" his ego."[37] But he emphasizes at the same time the tendencies of children in this age group, according to their growing abilities to watch, to join, to observe, and to participate. This can happen at school, in the street, at a friend's house, or at home. In this respect, the play assumes a quite important function: Contrary to an adult's play, which serves relaxation purposes, it allows the child a new level of coping with reality[38], "(…) an infantile way of mastering social experience by experimenting, planning, and sharing, alone and with playmates."[39]

Hence, for the child as opposed to the adult, play is not a means to flee reality, but rather a mechanism to cope with reality, which is increasingly important to the child. The play alone, however, is according to Erikson not enough for the development. The child wants to be useful and accomplish something, he develops pleasure in knowledge, determination, precision, perfection, and endurance, and he wants to create something.

During this stage, the child discovers that he can easily garner appreciation from others by learning or making things on his own. The acknowledgement tied to success is a motivation to be industrious and to work out things independently, which nurtures the sense of industry.

However, there is also the risk that failure could dampen a child's self-confidence. If there is no constant effort from the part of persons like teachers or parents, who have the function of a role model, to encourage another try, then these initial failures can evolve into a lasting inferiority complex.

In this stage, the child learns to earn recognition by accomplishing something.

In particular, when it comes to gaining recognition, another risk for the development of the child's identity is evident. "If the overly conforming child accepts work as the only criterion

[34] see ERIKSON, Identity. Youth and crisis, p.127
[35] see ERIKSON, Identity. Youth and crisis, p.125
[36] ERIKSON, Identity. Youth and crisis, p.122
[37] ERIKSON, Identity. Youth and crisis, p.122
[38] ERIKSON, Identity. Youth and crisis, p.123
[39] ERIKSON, Identity. Youth and crisis, p.123

of worthwhileness, sacrificing imagination and playfulness too readily (…)"[40], there is the risk of an emerging exaggerated industry effect and consequently of raising an easily exploitable conformist.

If during this stage, the child experiences events of success, entrusted responsibility, positive role assignment, and not continuous frustration, fear-inducing teaching methods (particularly in school), and exclusively performance-driven acceptance, then he can successfully overcome the crisis in this phase.
Consequently, his capabilities and positive attitude are fostered and feelings of inferiority and shortcoming are banned.

Erikson considers this stage as socially most decisive, "since industry involves doing things beside and with others, a first sense of division of labor and of differential opportunity (...) develops at this time."[41]

2.5   Identity vs. role confusion

Rapid body growth and genital maturity constitute crisis potential in the fifth stage, from puberty to about eighteen years of age. This stage corresponds to the genital phase (Freud) and includes the search for identity. Erikson talks of "almost a way of life between childhood and adulthood."[42]
A sustainable and stable self-identity can only take hold, if the crises in the earlier stages have been constructively resolved.
Self-identity allows the adolescent to understand himself as a personality embedded and accepted in society, who is, due to his acquired capabilities, equipped to face the challenges of the future.

Erikson sees the main reason for adolescent anxiety in the problem of choosing a professional identity.[43]
The young person is primarily interested in consolidating his social role and in being concerned with "(…) what they appear to be in the eyes of others as compared with what they

---

[40] ERIKSON, Identity. Youth and crisis, p.127
[41] ERIKSON, Childhood and Society, p. 260
[42] ERIKSON, Identity. Youth and Crisis, p.128
[43] see ERIKSON, Identity, Youth and Crisis, p.129

feel they are, and with the question of how to connect the roles and skills cultivated earlier with the occupational prototypes of the day"[44], meaning to develop a sense of identity. Questions appear as to what about the SELF and to "How am I seen by others?"

The distinct elements an adolescent has developed in preceding stages, like trust, autonomy, initiative, and industriousness, which are joined to a whole in this stage, are the more important, as they build an identity within society.

When during puberty the own body changes radically, the old values are questioned again, as the adolescent goes through a similar phase of upheaval like the infant.

In addition, there is the need for recognition from the outside, though for now recognition by peers is of prime importance, and to a lesser extent by parents or teachers.

Erikson calls this particularly critical and for the adolescent mostly confusing stage, the moratorium[45]. It implies that all options learned so far could be tried again during the waiting period of puberty, in order that the adolescent can be really sure at the end of this stage having chosen the personally best aspects for his personality.

In contrast to this is the assumption of a negative identity, respectively role confusion. Here the goal is to find the own identity through the negation of generally accepted values and norms.

"It is important to understand in principle (...) that such intolerance may be, for a while, a necessary defense against a sense of identity loss."[46]

Erikson describes role confusion as a conflict within the own personality, which simply cannot find out, if one is a real man (a real woman), if one can ever discern a purpose in the self and appear likeable, if one will be able to control oneself, if one will ever know for sure who he is, what he will be, how others will see him, and if one will ever grasp making the right decisions.[47]

"The danger of this state is role confusion. Where this is based on a strong previous doubt as to one's sexual identity, delinquent and outright psychotic episodes are not uncommon."[48]

In the ideal case, the moratorium is a transient state, which when overcome produces a grounded individual, who identifies with idols and ideas and sees a perspective and a future

---

[44] ERIKSON, Childhood and Society, p.261
[45] see ERIKSON, Childhood and Society, p.262
[46] ERIKSON, Identity, Youth and Crisis, p.132
[47] ERIKSON, Childhood and Society, p.261f.
[48] ERIKSON, Childhood and Society, p.262

for himself. Moreover, the own profession can be seen as an identity aspect and hence practiced with satisfaction.

When puberty comes to an end, under positive circumstances this leads to a successful development of identity. This implies that all acquired parts of the personality puzzle come together as a whole, which now makes up the personal identity. Hence, the young adult is able to live in harmony with himself and his environment, since he is cognizant of his inner stability and continuity.

An adolescent being cast by his environment as the born rascal, the strange bird, or outcast, often is driven by defiance to fulfill this prophecy.[49]

For this very reason it is particularly important for adults to unconditionally and in earnest acknowledge his real exploits, to exhibit a high degree of tolerance, confidence in his abilities and acceptance of his being the way he is, in order to enable him to master this crisis and to enter the next stage with an emboldened attitude.

Puberty is the stage, when the development of identity is experienced as particularly accentuated, while the formation of identity in itself is a lifelong process.

The defined identity is a precondition for intimacy, the development of which shall be the focus of the next stage.

2.6   Intimacy and dissociation from self-centeredness

The sixth stage takes place in early adulthood, when a young person did begin to work or study, and the encounter with the opposite gender is getting more serious, when marriage and the start of a family become imminent or have just begun.

With successfully going through the previous stage, personality formation is largely completed.

The central theme of this stage is the evolving of the capability for intimacy, the building of sustainable relationships, which is not restricted to heterosexual romantic relationships, but includes regular friendships as well. These intimate friendships among young people help, for

---

[49] ERIKSON, Identity, Youth and Crisis, p.132

example through conversations, to find the own viewpoint and often arise from "(…) the deep need of youth to redefine its identity (…)"[50].

The young person can commit himself to a relationship without having to fear a close attachment, which could result in merging the own identity with the partner's. Rather a relationship offers the opportunity to find the own self in the partner and to definitely get lost in the vis-a-vis for some time and with no risk, as this is the case in the sexual act for example. A tight relationship demands above all dependability and a sense of duty towards the partner.

Erikson elaborates,"body and ego must now be the masters of the organ modes and of the nuclear conflicts, in order to be able to face the fear of ego loss in situations which call for self-abandon: in the solidarity of close affiliations, in orgasms and sexual unions, in close friendships and in physical combat, in experiences of inspiration by teachers and of intuition from the recesses of the self."[51]

One has to comprehend, "(…) it is only when identity formation is well on its way, that true intimacy – which is really a counterpointing as well as a fusing of identities – is possible."[52]

Erikson mentions an "ethical sense"[53], which he calls the mark of the adult, which competitive encounter, the erotic bond, and merciless enmity are subjected to and which takes over from the ideological conviction of adolescence and the moralism of childhood.

Psychoanalysis has emphasized genitality as one of the developmental conditions for a healthy personality.[54] And according to Freud genitality implies the following:

"1. Mutuality of orgasm

2. with a loved partner

3. of the other sex

4. with whom one is able and willing to share a mutual trust

5. and with whom one is able and willing to regulate the cycles of

 a) work

 b) procreation

 c) recreation

6. so as to secure to the offspring, too, all the stages of satisfactory development."[55]

---

[50] ERIKSON, Childhood and Society, p.263
[51] ERIKSON, Childhood and Society, p.263
[52] ERIKSON, Identity, Youth and Crisis, p.135
[53] ERIKSON, Childhood and Society, p.264
[54] ERIKSON, Identity, Youth and Crisis, p.136

If such intimate relations are avoided, it can be expected that this being's future relationships will be distanced and calculating. "Where a youth does not acccomplish such intimate relationships with others (...) in late adolescence or early adulthood, he may settle for highly stereotyped interpersonal relations and come to retain a deep sense of isolation."[56]

The healthy counterpart of intimacy is distantiation, "(...) the readyness to isolate and, if necesary, to destroy those forces and people whose „territory" seems to encroach on the extent of one's intimate relations."[57] This more mature and effective way of rejecting has outgrown the blind prejudices of puberty.

Where the ability to identity and therefore to intimacy has not been developed sufficiently, the consequence is often isolation leading to psychic disorders, depressive self-absorption, or vulnerable characters.

Freud was once asked the question, what a person had to be able to do well, and was reported to have answered, "Lieben und Arbeiten" (to love and to work)[58]. Erikson adding, "thus we may ponder, but we cannot improve on ‚the professor's' formula."[59] At the same time, this includes doctor's orders for human dignity – and for a democratic way of life.

2.7   Generativity vs. Stagnation

According to Erikson, generativity encompasses two partner's desire to procreate and take parental responsibility.
For this reason the seventh stage, which a person experiences in mid-adulthood, is closely related to the problem of genitality.
Sexual partners, who in their relationship with each other find true genitality, will soon desire to raise with joint efforts a mutual offspring.[60]
The person having found his identity and intimacy in mid-adulthood can now devote oneself to caring for others.

---

[55] ERIKSON, Childhood and Society, p.266
[56] ERIKSON, Identity, Youth and Crisis, p.135
[57] ERIKSON, Childhood and Society, p.264
[58] ERIKSON, Identity, Youth and Crisis, p.136
[59] ERIKSON, Childhood and Society, p.265
[60] ERIKSON, Childhood and Society, p.266

Erikson calls this desire striving for generativity, since it does focus on the next generation through genitality and the genes.

However, as in previous stages, a prerequisite is the achievement of a positive and intact sense of identity. Instead of taking, now the need to give develops. Erikson states that, evolution has made man a learning, as well as a teaching animal, for dependency and maturity are reciprocal.[61] "(...) Maturity needs guidance as well as encouragement from what has been produced and must be taken care of."[62]

In "Identity: Youth and Crisis" he describes this seventh stage in even stronger terms. "And indeed, the concept of generativity is meant to include productivity and creativity, neither of which, however, can replace it as designations of a crisis in development. For the ability to lose oneself in the meeting of bodies and minds leads to a gradual expansion of ego-interests and to a libidinal investment in that which is being created."[63]

The concept of generativity, establishing and guiding the next generation, encompasses productivity as well as the creative giftedness, meaning that there are individuals who for whatever reasons do not apply this "drive"[64] to their own offspring, but to other forms of altruistic concern and hence achieve and secure continuity of their person beyond death, as for example through art or literature.

So, many people remain unmarried or have no children of their own, but want to do their part in the advancement of society, which in turn enriches their lives; in this way, not only the father fulfills his father function towards the child, but in reverse, the child affects the man.

Where this life goal cannot be reached, there is a risk of social isolation and alienation. The person meets others with hatred and hostility in an effort to protect himself.

"(...) Regression to an obsessive need for pseudointimacy takes place, often with a pervading sense of stagnation, boredom, and interpersonal impoverishment."[65]

Hereby, with an exaggerated desire to be alone, the person tries to forget his problems, by avoiding exposure to the impression of the so-called "happy family" as much as possible. At this juncture, individuals often begin to excessively indulge themselves as if they were their own child.

---

[61] ERIKSON, Identity, Youth and Crisis, p.138
[62] ERIKSON, Childhood and Society, p.267
[63] ERIKSON, Identity, Youth and Crisis, p.138
[64] ERIKSON, Identity, Youth and Crisis, p.138
[65] ERIKSON, Identity, Youth and Crisis, p.138

The mere fact of being married and having children does not necessarily imply generativity. Erikson points out that many young parents seem to suffer from the inability of developing this stage.[66] "The reasons are often to be found in early childhood impressions; in faulty identifications with parents; in excessive self-love based on a too strenuously self-made personality; and in the lack of some faith, some "belief in the species", which would make a child appear to be a welcome trust."[67]

2.8   Integrity vs. Despair and Disgust

Only who went through all seven previous stages, can now as an older adult complete this eighth stage by accepting the own life cycle the way it did present itself, including the people he encountered and the nature of these encounters.

Erikson names integrity as being the "fruit"[68] of the seven stages.

Ego integrity is finally the crowning, the synthesis of all parts. One has evolved, is able to accept and acknowledge the environment, is ready to stand up for the continuity of the own family; one has assumed a form of integrity and becomes a part of the whole, a link of the chain.

"Although aware of the relativity of all the various life styles which have given meaning to human striving, the possessor of integrity is ready to defend the dignity of his own life style against all physical and economic threats. For he knows that an individual life is the accidental coincidence of but one life cycle with but one segment of history; and that for him all human integrity stands or falls with the one style of integrity of which he partakes."[69]

Thus, it depends on how a person looks back on his past life and what kind of conclusion he draws. On the one hand, with this recap many past experiences prove meaningful, but on the other hand problems and life tasks reappear that have not been solved or couldn't, maybe were even suppressed.

The lack or loss of the accrued ego integration is signified by despair and by disgust. A possible outcome is senile despair, which can result from the realization that the own life may have failed and cannot be undone and one is overcome by a sense of worthlessness and

---

[66] see ERIKSON, Identity, Youth and Crisis, p.138
[67] ERIKSON, Identity, Youth and Crisis, p.138
[68] ERIKSON, Identity, Youth and Crisis, p.139
[69] ERIKSON, Childhood and Society, p.268

despondency, if no effort for trust or other things was made, be it through active or passive means.

Death appears as senseless finale and cannot be accepted as unalterable fate and is lamented with anxiety and fear of death.

" (...) the one and only life cycle is not accepted as the ultimate of life. Despair expresses the feeling that the time is now too short for the attempt to start another life and to try alternate roads to integrity (...)" and so " (...) signify the individual's contempt of himself."[70]

Erikson adds that the person faces a new edition of an identity crisis, which may be stated in the words "I am what survives of me."[71]

Such dispositions as faith, will power, purposefulness, competence, fidelity, love, care, wisdom, now flow " into the life of institutions."[72]

The human personality develops according to an innate plan; an inner strength inside, which at certain times in life confronts us with various conflicts of social interaction in order to enrich the individual as well as society.

"Psychosocial strength, we conclude, depends on a total process which regulates individual life cycles, the sequence of generations, and the structure of society simultaneously: for all three have evolved together."[73]

---

[70] ERIKSON, Identity, Youth and Crisis, p.140
[71] ERIKSON, Identity, Youth and Crisis, p.141
[72] see ERIKSON, Identity, Youth and Crisis, p.141
[73] ERIKSON, Identity, Youth and Crisis, p.141

3. Epigenetic Diagram of a System of Stages

	1	2	3	4	5	6	7	8	
I Infancy	Basic Trust vs. Mistrust				Unipolarity vs. Premature Self-differentiation				I. Infanc
II Early Childhood		Autonomy vs. Shame and Doubt			Bipolarity vs. Autism				II. Early Child
III Play Age			Initiative vs. Guilt		Play-Identification vs. (oedipal) Phantasy-Identities				III. Play A
IV School Age				Industry vs. Inferiority	Work-identification vs. Identity-blockage				IV. Schoc Age
V Adolescence	Temporal Perspective vs. Time Confusion	Self-Certainty vs. Painful Self-Consciousness	Role Experimentation vs. Negative Role Fixation	Apprenticeship vs. Work Paralysis	Identity vs. Role Confusion	Sexual Polarization vs. Bisexual Confusion	Leader- and Followership vs. Autority Confusion	Ideological Commitment vs. Confusion of Values	V Adolecence
VI Young Adulthood					Solidarity vs. Social Isolation	Intimacy vs. Isolation			VI Young Adult
VII Adulthood							Generativity vs. Stagnation		VII Adult
VIII Maturity								Ego Integrity vs. Despair	VIII Matur

3.1   Commentary

The highlighted boxes building a diagonale show the succession of psychosocial crises of the distinct developmental stages. The boxes contain the distinct criteria of relative psychosocial health and the corresponding psychosocial disorder.

With a "normal" development, the criterion of psychosocial health dominates, whereas the criterion of psychosocial disorder never is completely suppressed. The succession of the distinctive stages, at the same time, corresponds to the developmental sequence of the components of a psychosocial personality.

Each component, as shown with vertical boxes, already exists in a certain form even before the "proper" stage, in which a specific psychosocial crisis arises and is met with an individual's respective maturity, as well as the anticipated requirements of the given society.[74] In this way, each component comes to its ascendence, meets its crisis, and finds its lasting solution towards the end of the stages mentioned, but remains logically connected with all components. Again, all of them are dependent on the time and pace not just of an individual's development, but also on the requirements of society.

At the completion of adolescence, identity is expressed stage-specifically; at this point, the identity problem has to find its integration as a relatively conflict-free, psychosocial compromise, or it will remain dormant and conflict-laden.[75]

The epigenetic diagram of a system of stages can be found in Erikson's work "Identity: Youth and Crisis" on page 94.

---

[74] ERIKSON, Identity. Youth and Crisis, p.95
[75] ERIKSON, Identity. Youth and Crisis, p.95

4. Conclusion

Erikson built his theory of epigenesis of identity on Freud's developmental model and herewith created one of the most renowned extensions and modifications thereof. Moreover, he connects the idea of development within the life cycle with that issue which is becoming the focus of personality development during adolescence: the development of the ego identity. Achieving ego identity is the general theme of his theory and for him consists in the tackling of requirements that result from the individual being embedded in a social order.

"Eine Entwicklungsaufgabe stellt ein Bindeglied dar im Spannungsverhältnis zwischen individuellen Bedürfnissen und gesellschaftlichen Anforderungen. (A developmental challenge presents a link in the tensions between individual needs and societal requirements.)"[76].

Extending the scheme by three stages of adulthood puts emphasis on the fact that development is a lifelong process. Crises are not perceived as disruptive factors, but as needing active and constructive solutions, which can impart the individual a position of strength, if this crisis is understood as a chance.

With the active handling of the crisis in one stage, a new balance is achieved, which is elevated to the next stage, respectively phase. Hence, development can only take place, when crises are actively and constructively resolved.

Despite of its great merits, critique is justified that in the same way time and society is subjected to change, so is Erikson's model. The essential features of the model are certainly applicable to human beings of today, but due to the constant advancement of societal values and opinions, the model would have to be revised in some points.

In Erikson's day it was usual to get married as an adult and eventuallly to have children. This topic is discussed in detail in the seventh stage, generativity vs. stagnation. However, in the course of time this viewpoint has changed in some cultures. For example in Western industrialized countries single-biographies and other choices of lifestyle are no rarity anymore.

---

[76] OERTER/MONTADA, Entwicklungspsychologie (Developmental Psychology), p.269

Moreover, it has to be scrutinized, if Erikson's theory in this respect does not just refer to heterosexual couples, which does raise the question about the universal validity for all people, as often claimed by Erikson himself, and its relevance in present time. Moreover, homosexuals belong to a group in society for which the characteristic of the seventh stage, namely procreation, poses a problem of a biological kind.

This should, however, not take away from Erikson's merit, but rather draw attention to different possibilities of interpretation.

In contrast to Sigmund Freud, Erikson did perceive development as a lifelong process and he did commit himself to researching the processes of socialization, thus advancing psychoanalysis and developmental psychology a significant step forward.

This work is meant to provide an overview of Erikson's stage model and to conceptionally present it. A critical analysis was not intended; there is no claim for completeness.

5. Literature

Erikson, Erik H.: Identity: Youth and Crisis. W. W. Norton & Company Inc., New York 968. Austen Riggs Monograph No.7. Library of Congress, United States, 1968.
[cited as: ERIKSON, Identity. Youth and Crisis]

Erikson, Erik H.: Childhood and Society. W. W. Norton & Company Inc., New York. Library of Congress, United States, 1963.
[cited as: ERIKSON, Childhood and Society]

Oerter, Rolf/Montada, Leo: Entwicklungspsychologie. (Developmental Psychology) 5th, completely revised edition. Beltz Verlage, Weinheim, Basel, Berlin, 2002.
[cited as: OERTER/MONTADA, Entwicklungspsychologie]

Cover image: pixabay.com

Lightning Source UK Ltd.
Milton Keynes UK
UKHW010709080721
386832UK00003B/601